THE
intuitive
principal

THE
intuitive
principal

A GUIDE TO LEADERSHIP

KAREN M. DYER
JACQUELINE CAROTHERS

CORWIN PRESS, INC.
A Sage Publications Company
Thousand Oaks, California

For information:

CORWIN
PRESS

Corwin Press, Inc.
A Sage Publications Company
2455 Teller Road
Thousand Oaks, California 91320
E-mail: order@corwinpress.com

Sage Publications Ltd.
6 Bonhill Street
London EC2A 4PU
United Kingdom

Sage Publications India Pvt. Ltd.
M-32 Market
Greater Kailash I
New Delhi 110 048 India

Printed in the United States of America

Library of Congress Cataloging-in-Publication Data

Dyer, Karen M.
    The intuitive principal: A guide to leadership / by Karen M. Dyer, Jacqueline Carothers.
        p. cm.
    Includes bibliographical references and index.
    ISBN 0-7619-7531-4 (cloth: alk. paper)
    ISBN 0-7619-7532-2 (pbk.: alk. paper)
    1. School principals—United States. 2. Educational
leadership—United States. 3. Intuition. I. Carothers, Jacqueline.
II. Title.
    LB2831.92 .D94 2000
    371.2'012'0973—dc21   00-008190

This book is printed on acid-free paper.

01   02   03   04   05   10   9   8   7   6   5   4   3   2

Corwin Editorial Assistant: Catherine Kantor
Production Editor: Nevair Kabakian
Editorial Assistant: Victoria Cheng
Typesetter/Designer: Barbara Burkholder

Contents

Preface

Most all of us have flown in an airplane and know that right before the doors are closed, a cabin attendant, ground personnel, or flight crew member will make an announcement about the destination of the plane. The conversation goes somewhat like this:

> Ladies and gentlemen, the final destination of this flight is St. Louis, with a stop in Los Angeles. If this is your plan, you are on the right plane. If not, please ring your call button immediately. Thank you for choosing to fly Heavenly Airlines.

If you are interested in learning how to access intuitive ways of knowing to improve your effectiveness as an educational leader, you are metaphorically speaking "on the right plane." If you are interested in stories and examples from leaders who have accessed their intuitive abilities to help them become better problem solvers, more creative decision makers, and better anticipators of outcomes and events, you are reading the right book.

The demands on the school administrator and other educational leaders continue to multiply exponentially. Many argue, and we agree, that often the job can be characterized as "just not doable." A solid administrator preparation program, continuing professional development, experience, and mentoring by others are absolutely necessary but, unfortunately, not sufficient. Leaders must be able to avail themselves of the support of supervisors and colleagues and the personal systems of sustenance that are provided by spouses, children, friends, coaches, ministers, and an occasional mental health practitioner. All these, coupled with good nutrition, exercise, daily affirmations, outside of work activities, as well as opportunities to reflect on practice, are variables that can positively contribute to a leader's success. Yet we are of the assumption that intuitive ways of knowing oneself regarding personal strengths, weaknesses, interests, inherent values and beliefs, and intuitive alertness are key factors that can enable an administrator who is just surviving to become one who is self-actualized in the role.

We came to write this book because of the many conversations that we have held with principals and other administrators throughout the years. When we asked, "How did you know to make that particular decision?" or "What made you behave in that manner?" we consistently heard, "I just knew." As we listened to their stories, we learned that the responses to situations were not based solely on previous experience, learnings taken away from an administrator preparation program or a master's or doctoral program, a journal article that had been read, or advice from a colleague or supervisor. Although all these influence the behaviors and decision-making capabilities of leaders, we realized that successful leaders are also intuitive leaders.

We have learned from our own research, our personal experiences as principals, and talks with numerous educators in myriad settings that intuition is not necessarily about revelation. Sometimes, intuition involves knowing what we already know by examining and expanding on two important factors: *environmental readings* and *files from the past.* Thus, the purpose of this book is to examine the ability to intuit—to perceive things without conscious reasoning—a skill that leaders have long accessed but seldom acknowledged as an approach for decision making. This book acknowledges the use of intuition as both a valid and a valued strategy for enhancing leadership roles.

Chapter 1 focuses on "Intuitive Ways of Knowing." It references research on intuition that includes information about the levels of intuitive input as well as different stages involved with intuitive explorations.

Chapter 2 explores "Developing Behaviors of Intuitive Leadership." Using several distinguishing behaviors as a frame, this chapter provides a plethora of stories about intuitive leaders who have successfully based their actions and decisions on their abilities to read the environment and access files from the past.

Chapter 3 provides insight into "Powerful Communication." Looking at several forms of communication that include listening, speaking, writing, body language, and silence, this chapter provides examples of how intuitive skill can be applied to practical situations involving the art of communication.

Chapter 4 discusses "Intuition and the Paradoxes of Leadership." Four major paradoxes are addressed: leader versus manager, autocrat versus indecisive decision maker, facilitator versus obstructor, and delegator versus leader-centered problem solver.

WHAT THIS BOOK IS NOT ABOUT

Neither of us is a student of the science and art of intuition. We do not claim in any way to have a deep understanding of how to discover, develop, or define intuition. For that information, we suggest that you consult such authors as Frances Vaughan, Marcia Emery, Laura Day, and Nancy Rosanoff. We have relied on their expertise to help frame and sometimes explain the powers of intuition.

We do not attempt to quantify (test) or qualify (explain) actions regarding whether they are examples of pure intuition. We do not label actions as examples of intuition versus impulsivity, intuition versus logic, intuition versus common sense, intuition versus wishful thinking, or intuition versus attitude. We leave that to others to define.

ACKNOWLEDGMENTS

We would like to thank the many educators (you know who you are, or maybe you don't) who shared their stories with us. To maintain confidentiality, we have changed names, circumstances, gender, timelines, settings, and so on. All the examples used are hybrids of several events that were related to us, occasionally accented with personal experiences and our own research.

We would also like to thank our respective families for their unconditional love and understanding. During the process of writing this book and always, they have supported our efforts by consistently reminding us to keep our eyes on the prize. We both are blessed with friends who have encouraged us via a kind word, a small note, or an admonishment to "stop the dance and get to work." We appreciate their understanding when we had to postpone getting together, shorten a phone conversation, or curtail visits and events that would have effected mutual pleasures.

Thank you to colleagues at the Chicago Academy for School Leadership, the Chicago Principals' and Administrators' Association, and Chicago Public Schools for allowing us to access their thinking, their time, and their talents. We also would like to express our appreciation to Pam Robbins and Kent Peterson for their advice and mentorship.

As always, the alpha and omega of our praise and appreciation go to the Father, Son, and Spirit, through whom all things are possible.

About the Authors

Karen M. Dyer, EdD, is Manager of the Education Sector for the Center for Creative Leadership. Prior to this position she was the Executive Director of the Chicago Academy for School Leadership, responsible for providing rigorous results-based professional development for Chicago Public School principals and administrators. Previous to this, she served as the Executive Director of the Bay Area and North Bay School Leadership Centers, both part of the California School Leadership Academy. She has been a principal, Title I program manager, reading/language arts specialist, teacher of regular and gifted education at both elementary and middle grades, and an instructor at California State University, Hayward and Nova University. Dr. Dyer has made presentations for the Association for Supervision and Curriculum Development (ASCD), the National Staff Development Council (NSDC), the National Association for Elementary School Principals (NAESP), the National School Boards Association (NSBA), the National Alliance for Black School Educators (NABSE), the National Board for Professional Teaching Standards (NBPTS), the College of William and Mary, and the comprehensive school reform program, Co-nect. She has done consultation work with school districts in Alaska, California, Illinois, Maryland, Mississippi, North Carolina, and Virginia. She is the author of numerous instructional leadership modules including *Principally Speaking: What Principals Need to Know About the National Board for Professional Teaching Stan-*

dards. She is also a featured expert on ASCD's video series, *The Principal*. She holds a bachelors degree from the University of California, Berkeley, a master of education degree from Holy Names College in Oakland, California, and a doctorate in education administration from the University of the Pacific in Stockton, California.

Jacqueline Carothers, EdD, is currently a Director for the Chicago Academy for School Leadership. Formerly, she served as principal of two elementary schools in the Chicago public schools system. She holds a bachelor's degree in English from the University of Illinois at Chicago, a master's of education degree in reading and learning disabilities from DePaul University in Chicago, a doctorate in school leadership from the University of Illinois at Champaign, and an Illinois Superintendent's Certificate. She has served as principal, Title I coordinator, Title I reading coordinator, master teacher, and elementary school teacher for intermediate and upper grades. A member of several organizations, she has made presentations at the National Assoication of Elementary School Principals, the Association for Supervision and Curriculum Development, the National Staff Development Council, the National Alliance of Black School Educators, the National School Boards Association, and the Chicago Alliance of Black School Educators. Her experiences as a staff developer include associations with Maryland and New York school districts, Chicago city colleges, and a number of other private schools and professional organizations. She is a Whitman Award winner. Recently, she conducted a professional development session (Principals' Workshop) in Germany for the U.S. Department of Defense Education Services and provided the keynote address for the Maryland State Department of Education's School Improvement Leadership Conference.

CORWIN
PRESS

The Corwin Press logo—a raven striding across an open book—represents the happy union of courage and learning. We are a professional-level publisher of books and journals for K-12 educators, and we are committed to creating and providing resources that embody these qualities. Corwin's motto is "Success for All Learners."

1

∿

Intuitive Ways of Knowing

Intuition is when you know something without knowing how you know it. Intuition is an internal guidance system which is part association and memory, part experience, and part unknown.

Nancy Rosanoff (1991, p. 16)

Effective leaders subconsciously access lessons learned from persons whom they admire or from actions that they respect. Significant information garnered through conversations, observations, readings, and so on is internalized. When a decision must be made, however, leaders do not stop and ask, "Is this a Bolman and Deal moment?" They do not rush off to their bookcases to retrieve and rifle through a copy of Michael Fullan's latest work in search of an appropriate solution. Although the importance of accessing pertinent research is acknowledged, theoretical or customary responses to dealing with problems do not present themselves as sources of paralysis in thinking or action. Leaders, those who are intuitive, access previously compartmentalized, relevant, and important thoughts that have been stored in their mental filing system through environmental readings, files from the past, or a combination thereof.

> A principal walking the halls sees two female students sitting on the floor outside a classroom. Both have pencils in hand and appear to be doing work. The principal has not had any prior interaction with the students and assumes that they are in the hall because of a class project. The principal acknowledges them with a nod and proceeds to her destination. Later on that day, two male students are sitting outside the same classroom, again with pencils in hand and appearing to do work. This time, the principal assumes that they are there because of a discipline matter and decides to question them.

Environmental Readings

Before actions are taken, the context of a situation is read—subconsciously noting the five "w's": *who, what, where, when,* and *why.* A 360-degree scan of the environment contributes to peripheral intuition—an ability to use all the senses to read more than what is simply within proximity. Environmental readings serve as source material for determining which mental file should be tapped.

In the former scenario, one could argue that this was a case of gender bias. Yet further conversation with the principal revealed that she was correct in her assessment of the hallway situation—the girls were working on a project, and the boys were there for discipline reasons. She was able to "intuitively" discern which situation called for intervention based on an environmental reading.

Files From the Past

Connecting to files from the past enables leaders to benefit from experiences that cannot immediately be identified or isolated. Intuitive leaders "just know the right thing to do" even if they do not remember how they "came to know it." Again, in reference to the previous example, the principal was able to access files from the past related to previous encounters with students—positive, negative, and neutral. Files from the past are also composed of prior conversations that may have had nothing to do with the students in question but more to do with the discipline patterns of the particular teacher. Other unrelated and even unconscious "files" may contribute to leaders' intuitive way of knowing.

Both our bodies and our minds are receptacles for an abundance of information. Feelings, thoughts, and impulses, no matter how vague or subtle, get registered in our brains and neuromuscular structures. Although the mind may not be consciously aware of all these internal and external stimuli of events and emotions, the body is registering all of them. Thus, the files from the past are not just simple recollections but giant data banks of stored memories, knowledge, and creativity.

Environmental readings coupled with files from the past almost instantaneously inform appropriate intuitive responses. As pointed out by Frances Vaughan (1979),

> If you are willing to become more conscious of your own beliefs and the alternatives you are intuitively aware of, you can begin to see that to a great extent your life as it is now is the result of choices you made in the past, and that your future will evolve according to the choices you are making now. . . . Making choices for your own growth, trusting your intuition, can become a habit.

FIVE LEVELS OF INTUITIVE INPUT

Knowing how to read the environment and access files from the past complements other studies on intuition. Vaughan (1979) and Emery (1994) have identified five levels of experience that can also serve as sources of intuitive inputs as one seeks to increase knowledge about self:

Physical (body)

Mental (mind)

Emotional (heart)

Spiritual (soul)

Environmental (place)

At the *physical* level, a tingling in the ear, butterflies in the stomach, an itching palm, or an eye twitch can trigger "getting the picture." One administrator talked about a dull pain in his lower back that he generally associates with an imminent call from the president of his district's board of trustees. On a positive note, an assistant principal claims that a type of sixth sense tells him that on those mornings when he naturally awakens without the assistance of his alarm clock, he can expect relatively calm lunchroom periods at the middle school where he works. There are no ends to the various tactile, kinesthetic, gustatory, olfactory, auditory, and/or visual cues that trigger our physical way of knowing.

Mentally, a "lightbulb going off" or an "aha," a vision, or an instant flash of knowing signals understandings that allow us to read situations and people or even anticipate a potential crisis. When the seemingly disparate puzzle pieces come together to make a coherent whole without the benefit of logical, commonsensical thought processing or even simple precedent, we know that the reservoir of memories, creativity, and wisdom located in our subconscious has surfaced.

A dean of students illustrated this when he spoke about an awkward situation involving a teacher and a student.

> The student claimed that the teacher had gotten angry and, out of the sight of witnesses, had struck him. The teacher calmly denied the accusation and reminded the dean that the student had been reprimanded for lying in the past. The dean went on to relate that he confronted the teacher, out of the presence of the student, with a simple statement, "I know that Geoffrey is not lying," followed by "Now, why don't you just tell me what really happened." The teacher eventually admitted that out of frustration, he had hit the student. When asked how he knew that the teacher was the one not telling the truth, the dean stated, "I just knew. The truth just 'popped into my head.'"

At the *emotional* level, cues are transmitted to or about someone else in the form of a feeling. Emery (1994) describes this as "an immediate like or dislike, sudden change of mood, or feeling extremely receptive or averse to someone without logical provocation" (p. 13). The most common example of operating at the emotional level relates to "first impressions" often manifested during employment interviews. It is often reported that one person has been chosen over another given that qualifications, experience, overall manner, and appearance are equal. Says one superintendent about the selection of an executive assistant:

> "I knew from the moment I saw the application. Although there was another candidate with similar background and even more experience, I just knew that Doreen would be a better complement to me and my style of working. And, after five years, I have never regretted my decision."

A principal described a somewhat romantic element as part of the emotional level:

> During a job fair, the principal recalled interviewing more than 35 teacher candidates, selecting three teachers to join her staff. In addition to being extremely impressed with the skill level of two of these novice teachers, the principal remembered that something else had struck her: "Wouldn't they make a cute couple." Neither of the teachers knew each other, as they had both lived and attended college in different states. Two years later, this principal offered the first toast at their wedding.

The *spiritual* level acknowledges that there is something greater than what is tangibly present in the physical world.

> After serving quite successfully as an assistant superintendent for more than five years, a 38-year-old colleague was a shoo-in for the superintendency. She was endorsed by both teachers' and classified employees' unions and by the retiring superintendent. Informal communication from board of trustees members indicated that the position would not be advertised and that it would be offered to the assistant. Shortly before the official announcement, the assistant telephoned the board president and told her that she would not be available to accept the position because she had recently signed up for a two-year stint in the Peace Corps.

Needless to say, most everyone was in a state of shock. Rumors were rampant until the assistant superintendent issued the following statement:

> "Recently, I announced that I have accepted a two-year position in the Peace Corps. I am excited about this new venture and ask that you keep me in your thoughts and prayers. Having grown up professionally in this district, serving as a teacher, a principal, and an assistant superintendent, I am both honored and humbled that so many

of you have endorsed me as the next superintendent. I have not taken this endorsement lightly. Yet having been blessed with so many gifts in my life—caring family, supportive friends, meaningful work, and good health—I have decided to take a temporary hiatus from a life and a career that have brought me so much joy to work with others that they may have an opportunity to create a similar reality for themselves. I have not turned my back on the students, parents, teachers, and staff of this wonderful school community. Rather, the lessons that I have learned from all of you are helping to propel me toward this new phase in my life. We all are "called" to serve in different capacities—as a parent, teacher, minister, doctor, etc. I have decided to accept the call to be a Peace Corps volunteer. Thank you for your understanding."

The *environmental* level of intuitive experience involves cues, clues, and signals from our physical surroundings. Emery (1994) describes this as the flat tire on your car that might be telling you not to go to a certain meeting. An electric outage that causes your computer to go down could be saying "It's time for vacation." Perhaps numerous attempts to contact someone by telephone signal that this is not the time to connect with that person.

A principal reported that she was most annoyed when, late for a meeting, she was stopped for speeding (doing 42 mph in a 35 mph zone) about a half mile from her school. While silently acknowledging that she had been rightfully stopped for violating the speed limit, she was nonetheless embarrassed when she noticed a group of her students on their way to school, walking in her direction. Peering in her rearview mirror, she noticed that the students, seeing the officer, ducked into an alley. After accepting the ticket and admonishment from the police officer, she walked over to the alley only to discover the crowd of students egging on two of their members to fight. Her presence scattered the crowd and averted the impending confrontation. Later, one of the students involved in the fight asked her, "How did you know to be there?" She replied, "I didn't know. It was a case of being in the right place at the right time" and, secretly to herself, "for the wrong reason."

Logical explanation or intuitive data received from environmental readings and files from the past—either or both could explain what was present in each of the scenarios used to illustrate the five levels of intuitive experience. What is known is that seldom is time

taken to thoroughly analyze all our behaviors to their rational con-
clusions. Research, however, does provide useful data when trying
to explain the how and why of certain intuitive actions and decisions.

INTUITIVE EXPLORATIONS

In the 1960s, Dr. Douglas Dean, along with his colleague, John
Mihalsky, tested approximately 165 presidents and CEOs of U.S.
companies and found that 80% of these leaders who had doubled or
more than doubled their company profits in a 5-year period had
above-average predictive computer test scores. (A predictive computer score is a measure of intuitive ability.) The results of this
research are chronicled in their book, *Executive ESP* (1974). The
results of these studies led Dean and Mihalsky to conclude that
"prophets make profits" (cited in Emery, 1994, p. 23). Further testing
found that dynamic people, those who tend to get 25 to 30 things
done in a day, had higher than average intuitive scores. The
nondynamic people, those who tend to procrastinate, had lower
than average scores.

On the basis of his study of more than 3,000 managers nation-
wide, Weston Agor (1986) discovered that top executives actually
use intuitive ability in their decision making. He details his findings
in *The Logic of Intuitive Decision Making* by identifying circumstances
in which intuition was most often used by those involved in this particular study:

- Where there is a high level of uncertainty
- Where there is little precedent
- Where variables are less scientifically predictable
- Where facts are limited
- Where facts do not clearly indicate the direction to take
- Where analytical data are of little use (e.g., an
  emerging trend)
- Where there are several plausible solutions
- Where time is limited and there is pressure to be right
- Where negotiations and personnel decisions are paramount

So what happens when leaders are confronted by one or more of
these variables? What are the intuitive tools that support them in

Figure 1.1. Intuitive Problem-Solving Formula

making the right decisions? Emery (1994), building on the work initiated by Dean and Mihalsky (1974) and Agor (1984), has created an intuitive problem-solving (IPS) formula that involves processes in which many leaders (often unconsciously) engage as they enact solutions to even the most challenging problems. Her IPS formula is composed of the following facets: in the silence, introspection, imagination, illumination, incubation, and implementation (Figure 1.1).

In the Silence

Many times, solutions can surface when one avails oneself of a quiet place where environmental stimuli are at a minimum. Physically divorcing oneself from tension, turmoil, stress, and negativity helps awaken one's intuition. Closing the office door may be a solution for some but not always the foremost solution for others because of an awareness of action that might be going on just outside the door. For site administrators, sometimes sitting in the car in the parking lot, making a quick trip to an empty classroom, taking a walk around the block, or simply finding a quiet spot in a gymnasium, cafeteria, storeroom, janitor's closet, or bathroom stall may provide the time to clear their heads so that solutions can emerge.

When physical detachment is impossible, gentle music or other relaxing sounds can serve as a medium for escape—just until the answer to a stubborn question or dilemma surfaces. For some, focused breathing or yoga or similar exercises—even done at the desk—can serve as a means to access periods of silence.

Introspection

A looking inward to thoughts, emotions, feelings, and files from the past may help a leader approach a problem or view a situation from a different perspective. The complexities, uncertainties, and occasional value conflicts inherent in the role of a 21st-century educational leader require a degree of self-examination and reflection. According to Schön (1989),

> There are times when people get stuck and want to get unstuck, or want to help someone else learn to do something, or want to build their own spontaneous artistry. . . . Then people become observers of their own on-the-spot experiments, reflect on what they observe, and try to describe their knowing, their inquiry, and their change in view. This reflective process can be likened to engaging in an internal dialogue with one's self using experience, intuition, and trial-and-error thinking in defining and solving a problem or dilemma.

In dealing with situations that involve novelty, instability, and uncertainty, a leader would do well to realize that time devoted to introspection is more of a long-term investment than a short-term expenditure. The act of introspection heightens the probability of a more satisfying solution occurring. Introspection also provides opportunities to awaken those files from the past.

Imagination

Imagination involves a belief or supposition that most likely is beyond the realm of traditional thought. Like creativity, imagination represents an ability to "give birth" to new ideas and new ways of looking at things. Imagination can spur a capacity for leaders to make novel connections between seemingly disparate events and situations. Its use also helps create solutions that might have been missed by a typical way of viewing a problem.

Unfortunately, the use of imagination is sometimes considered a childlike act—inappropriate for adults. As Thomas Armstrong (1998) points out, imagination, for adults, has come to be associated with something negative (e.g., daydreaming) rather than being viewed as a potential source of cognitive power. When convention gives way to novel images, words, actions, and ideas, however, intuition is unleashed.

Imagination is not limited to visual imagery. According to Emery (1994), it can encompass a voice, a feeling, a "taste" for the answer, "sniffing" out the solution, or just knowing what direction one should take. Imagination can occur passively or spontaneously or come in the form of an impression, a number, a picture, a metaphor, a symbol, or a familiar word or phrase.

Illumination

Illumination involves interpreting the imagery as well as other environmental cues. Often, one can "read" a solution by being in tune with the physical and emotional feedback that comes via an examination of the situation. When Agor (1986) interviewed top executives and managers about their decision-making practices, he reported that many described feelings of excitement, a "bolt of lightning," or a solution that came as a "sudden flash." When decisions were not correct, respondents talked about "senses of anxiety," "mixed signals," "sleepless nights," and "upset stomachs." As we detailed at the beginning of the chapter, environmental readings and files from the past are illuminating modes for problem solving and decision making.

Incubation

Sometimes, the best way to come to a solution is to take leave of it—for a while. Often, it helps to establish time and space between you and the problem so that in the interim, the well of ideas is replenished. Wishful thinking, fear, anxiety, fatigue, and depression are signals that it is time to get away from the problem. Even after resolution is reached, a resting or incubation period can provide time to access logical thought processes or even intuition—whatever will lead to the right decision.

Implementation

Once intuition has provided a solution, it is time to activate it. Many times, however, because leaders are wanting in trust in intuitive problem solving, they will hesitate to implement decisions that may not have come through verbal, logical, and/or analytical channels.

The following case is an example of how the different facets of the intuitive problem-solving formula dynamically work toward actualizing a solution.

A newly appointed principal, Ron, discovered two weeks after the start of school that one of his assistant principals had taken a job in a neighboring district. Seeing this as an opportunity to shape the culture to be more focused on teaching and learning and on higher expectations for students, Ron felt that the hiring of a new co-administrator would probably be one of the most important tasks in his tenure at the school. Ron was determined to choose a person who was willing to be an integral part of this vision.

After advertising and interviewing several applicants, the selection committee recommended two candidates. The first was a counselor who had worked at the school for 22 years and had a reputation for being a "perennial applicant"—always applying for open administrative positions. The second was a popular teacher and former student who had recently received his administrative certification. Both candidates interviewed well; each presented a compelling case for being selected for the position. Ron was especially impressed by the counselor. Her reputation was troubling to him, however, and remained in the forefront of his mind. The popular teacher appeared to be the logical choice—but still something was not "quite right."

Although he seldom took a formal lunch break, Ron decided that he needed some quiet time (in the silence). He drove to a nearby fast-food restaurant, went through the drive-through, parked in a remote section of the lot, ate his lunch, and pondered his decision. Closing his eyes, he reflected for a while on his own transition from teacher to administrator (introspection). He thought about other hiring decisions that he had made in the past—successful ones as well as those he wished he could reverse. As he headed back to school, he noticed a billboard advertising a new cellular service. For a moment, he visualized a cell phone programmed to automatically dial a "solution hotline" (imagination). The solution hotline somehow made him think of his own children, who as toddlers, would use their toy phones to "call up" people, real and imaginary, who were always available to talk. He smiled as he recalled being called to the phone by one of his children to "chat" with an imaginary friend. For some reason, Ron thought that maybe an informal chat with each of the candidates would provide him with different information to help in his decision making (illumination).

On his return, Ron quickly discovered why he seldom took lunch breaks away from campus. There had been some problems in a substitute teacher's classroom, and three students were in his office waiting to see him. Under his breath, he sighed, "So much for hiring decisions," and consciously relegated thoughts about the two candidates to the back of his mind as he attended to the situation at hand (incubation).

After school, Ron asked both candidates to meet with him. He explained that the choice was down to the two of them and that he wanted to learn more about them during an informal chat. For approximately 30 minutes, the three of them sat and talked. Their discourse focused mostly on the school, where it had been, and where they thought it should go. Ron tried as much as possible to steer the conversation so that it was more between the two of them and less with him. Observing their interaction, Ron noticed that the teacher often deferred to the counselor, readily agreeing with her, sometimes reiterating the same opinion. At first, Ron thought that it was simply a sign of respect. He realized, however, that this behavior may have been what had been bothering him. The teacher seemed more inclined to give an "appropriate" answer—but seldom initiated an opinion that was uniquely his own. After this meeting, Ron knew which person he would choose.

Although Emery and others suggest that many responses are automatic, the more that one can learn about personal "recipes" for solving problems, the better one can make use of the tools of intuition. Intuitive leadership is less about content and more about the context. It involves taking an experience or event and, without hesitation or detailed thought, automatically sifting it through a sieve of environmental readings and files from the past. The effective leader "knows" what to do because there is an implicit trust in the data

gleaned from a storage bin of common sense, prior training, pro-
cessed patterns, peripheral perceptions, and physiological
interactions.

The following chapter addresses those behaviors that distin-
guish leaders who just respond from those who intuitively act.

2

Developing Behaviors of
Intuitive Leadership

Effective leaders intuitively engage in practices that have come to serve as distinguishing behaviors.

1. They are not paralyzed by timing.
2. They do not wait for permission to act.
3. They understand the importance of shared values.
4. They recognize that the culture of trust once violated is difficult to restore.
5. They are visionary.
6. They recognize that sharing leadership expands capacity.
7. They are willing to collaborate with others both like and unlike themselves.
8. They balance personal and positional power within the political context.

Throughout this chapter, examples of these distinguishing behaviors will be shared through stories collected from leaders who comfortably access their intuitive powers.

Leaders for the 21st century must view leadership through the lens of its effect on actions of staff members that subsequently affect student achievement. Concepts formerly associated with effective leadership must constantly be reexamined. The application of the concept of intuition and the associated influences of files from the past and environmental readings can provide valuable constructs for examining leadership.

TIMING

Intuitively recognizing the significance of and leverage to be gained from timing is an important distinguishing behavior. Timing can significantly affect the success or failure of actions taken. Much too often, organizational leaders decide to restructure roles, relationships, or procedures without paying attention to cultural clues in the environment that clearly say, "Don't go there."

A principal described an incident that illustrated how he benefited from paying careful attention to timing:

> He had been assigned to his school at midyear. Intuitively recognizing the importance of timing, he chose to hold off making changes that did not immediately affect issues related to the health and safety of children. This principal recognized that because the staff, parents, and the students had experienced nine changes in leadership in five years, they had "survived by doing their own thing." Continuous changes in focus had forced them to individually make accommodations that governed their interactions, specifically in the area of a particular grading policy.
>
> The principal was able to use as leverage excessive numbers of complaints from parents made during the third and final marking periods to substantiate the need for a schoolwide grading policy. During the first faculty meeting of the new school year, the principal shared a series of hair-raising anecdotes about teachers lacking the ability to produce grade books or to document the content of assignments that served as the basis for grades. Although staff mem-

bers voiced numerous complaints about proposed format require-
ments and deadlines, the concept of the need for a formalized policy
could not be effectively challenged.

In the previous scenario, an intuitive application of appropriate
timing crucially effected the acceptance of change. The procedural
change in local norms resulted in the establishment of a consistent
policy for evaluating students' academic progress. This action was
the first in a series of accountability measures aimed at reshaping the
culture of the school.

PERMISSION TO ACT

Competent and confident leaders are generally sensitive to situations in which failure to act would be synonymous with the abdica-
tion of responsibility. Such leaders assume responsibility for constantly promoting the actualization of a vision of academic success
for all students even when all constituents do not immediately buy
into that vision. Intuitively, such leaders consistently maintain a
mental picture of their ultimate goal. They are not constrained by
having to "know how they know." Instead, they act, acknowledging
their willingness to revise the actions if they do not like the results.
For those assertive leaders, staff and students alike recognize that
linking actions to a vision serves as the "why" that gives permission
to act. Consequently, with the expectation that there will be converts
and/or mistakes made, intuitive leaders rarely avoid initiating an
action that their intuition identifies as supportive of their vision of
academic excellence.

A leader who envisioned technology as the vehicle for enhancing the
instructional program began to identify and tap resources and experiences that she viewed as vital. She had attended a technology conference and had left convinced that the integration of technology
into the math and science curriculum could serve as the basis for
ultimately raising achievement scores. Although district funding was
not available, she immediately contacted and began a series of
exploratory conversations with a major distributor of computer
hardware and software. She ultimately requested an opportunity to

bring her school's entire faculty and parents to an information session at the home office of the company where the possibilities of using technology to enhance teaching and learning could best be explored.

During the session, the faculty was asked to view a variety of technological applications and to reflect on whether any of the solutions could effectively address the instruction-related needs of the students. The audience left the workshop impressed with the possibilities for change but frustrated by the lack of availability of immediate funding to support the integration of technology and instruction. Instead of waiting, the principal moved forward, identifying staff members who were willing to write grants and/or to be trained to use the new technology. As grants were won and budgets were realigned, instructional technology was incrementally introduced into the school several years before the school district began to provide financial support.

IMPORTANCE OF SHARED VALUES

Effective leaders intuitively recognize the importance of and seek opportunities for dialoguing with staff, students, and community members about the values that support their vision for teaching and learning. Every event or action is intuitively cataloged and quickly analyzed (files from the past) for its benefit as an opportunity for reinforcing accepted values.

One principal's past participation with a church group led him to decide that acts of kindness could be encouraged through the creation of a vine of kindness. Faculty, staff, students, and parents were permitted to add a leaf to the vine in recognition of another person's random act of kindness. By midyear, the vine of kindness could be seen spreading throughout the corridors. In their quest to have their names appear on the vine, both children and adults became more conscious of how they treated each other. As the vine continued to grow, the climate in the building began to change. Respectful dialogues, sharing, and collaboration began to surface as norms of expected behavior.

CULTURE OF TRUST

Discerning principals are conscious of subtle reactions to their actions that negatively affect school climate. They recognize that their staff members, parents, and students carefully observe whether the actions of the leaders are consistent with their espoused values. These leaders view reading the culture as essential to understanding the groundwork needed to support positive change. As change agents, leaders must have "a true understanding of cultural dynamics and the properties of their own organizational culture" (Schein, 1996, p. 64). The challenge for the leader is that of constantly focusing attention not only on what is happening but also on the underlying message. Actions are taken in response to environmental readings taken through the senses.

Like culture,

> Intuition is often symbolic and fragmentary. . . . Your intuition is so deeply interwoven in your other mental processes that you can no longer use it independently of your thoughts, feelings, knowledge, and seemingly logical decision making processes. Just as logic can be clouded by feelings, intuition can be clouded by knowledge and logic. (Day, 1997, p. 50)

Nothing that happens within a school is without meaning.

Intuitive leaders acknowledge that staff members expect that once rules and procedures are expressed by the leader as policy, those who comply will be rewarded or be safe from attack. A principal shared the story of why one of his staff members expressed a reluctance to participate in a pilot instructional program:

> That teacher related a negative experience with risk taking. The experience had occurred at that school under another principal's administration. The teacher had asked for and received the principal's permission to deviate from a district mandate. Nevertheless, when by way of an irate parent, news of the deviation reached the district office, the principal castigated the teacher for causing problems. Word of this attack quickly passed from teacher to teacher. Subsequently, staff began to refuse to take risks unless the principal gave written permission. The current principal intuitively responded to the issue of lack of trust by including within faculty bulletins statements that identified risk takers and celebrated the professional risks that were undertaken. That leader demonstrated that paying attention to people's needs was a powerful tool for gaining commitment. The principal and the school reaped the benefits of environmental readings taken as he watched, sensed, listened, and interpreted. (Deal & Peterson, 1999)

Another leader related an incident illustrating a negative impact:

> A colleague was known for sharing personal stories that had been related to him in confidence. This particular person made the mistake of sharing intimate details of a conversation with a staff member who actually knew the subject of conversation. Word got back to the teacher in question, and an ugly encounter occurred within hearing range of others. Needless to say, that person's credibility was diminished.

Intuitive leaders recognize that confidences are never violated. Those leaders view trust as a source of power.

***

VISION

Effective leaders walk with their heads held high in the clouds of vision, but their feet are firmly grounded in the realities of recognizing and orchestrating scenarios during which their vision can be actualized. Intuitive leaders remain constantly alert to the need to shape conditions in support of creating optimum circumstances under which all students can and will learn. At one school, the leader requires that teachers include within each of their lesson designs a variety of instructional and assessment strategies. Drawing on multiple strategies acknowledges the potential for reaching students that can be expanded through the use of technology, learning styles and multiple intelligences theories, traditional and performance assessment strategies, portfolios, and so forth. Staff members are encouraged to experiment with new practices. Intuitive leaders facilitate the structuring of opportunities that encourage reflection, discussion, and debate. Visits by teachers to other schools provide valuable opportunities to observe practice and for dialogue across communities.

Intuitively, effective leaders continuously recognize and promote opportunities to build strong professional communities that use knowledge, experience, and research to improve practice. The inherent value of encouraging teachers to self-select professional development activities that meet their personal needs was mentioned by a number of principals. In those schools, periodically throughout the year, teachers are provided with time during which they report on their new or validating learning experiences. Department and grade-level meetings focus on teaching and learning.

Areas in which student achievement is marginal become the focus of professional development. Staff members are encouraged to rely on both theory and action research as sources for improving practice. Professional development initiatives actually provide the support and create the opportunities needed to promote the maintenance of "a community of learners."

SHARING LEADERSHIP

Intuitive leaders recognize that their confidence in the capacity of others can be a constant source of leverage for actualizing their personal visions. They eagerly buy into the concept of the "de-jobbing of organizations" that William Bridges (1996) postulates as a major feature of the new concept of leadership. "Leadership passes back and forth from person to person as phases of the project succeed one another and different skills become critical" (p. 15). By sharing leadership, intuitive leaders are able to balance continuity and improvement.

> A principal told of being asked by a visitor, "How do you do all that you do?" The principal's response was, "That's an easy question to answer—I don't do it all." That principal shared that early in his tenure as a principal, he recognized that this was a "killer job." After spending some time engaging in periods of very personal and private reflections, he accepted that there was no one right way to be a principal or to solve any problem. Instead, he saw the need to build a strong professional community that used a combination of intuitive knowledge, experiences, and research to improve practice.
>
> While never losing sight of his personal vision for teaching and learning, the principal intuitively stepped aside and assumed the role of facilitator of the leadership of leaders. In doing so, the principal did not do as so many other leaders do—prevent staff members who were potential successors from having the types of experiences that would prepare them to become principals.

This successful leader was at the stage in his professional development where he had "enough personal insight to grow with the organization and change [his] own outlook or recognize [his] own limitations and permit other forms of leadership to emerge" (Schein, 1996, p. 63).

> At one school, the annual school improvement planning process is used as a vehicle for sharing leadership. Every responsibility and

activity listed in the plan become opportunities for sharing leadership. Teacher leaders chair departments or grade levels, sponsor clubs, facilitate special competitions, plan assemblies, and lead committees. All staff members are expected to participate as facilitators of at least two activities. This intuitive principal bases her assignments on lessons learned as she listens for and responds to the observable interests of staff members. Staff members expect that opportunities to serve as a leader will eventually be provided for everyone. Consequently, this anticipation of leading has led them to become more cooperative. A competitive spirit around the creation of excellence has served as an impetus for continuous improvement.

The task of the leader is to make sure that the individuals or groups are competent to exercise the responsibility that is given to them, understand the goals of the organization, and are committed to them. (Handy, 1996, p. 5)

The absence of confidence in the ability of others limits output.

An elementary school principal shared a decision that was grounded in her confidence in the connection between expressed desire and subsequent outcome. In this instance, the principal had made a decision to restructure the assignment of teachers to first-grade classrooms. This was done to circumvent the stifling control that was being exerted over grade-level colleagues by an award-winning teacher. The situation was complicated because the principal had publicly committed to a new organizational chart from which there were to be no deviations. Several days later, the principal was notified that her most successful kindergarten teacher was seriously ill and would not return to work. The principal had no backup plan in mind. Ironically, that same day, the least senior first-grade teacher approached the principal and asked to be assigned to the pending vacancy.

    The principal recalled her edict that first-grade teachers would all be assigned to new first-grade classrooms. Intuitively, however, she felt that changing this teacher from first grade to kindergarten was the appropriate thing to do. She abruptly decided to rescind her original plan. As the year progressed, that teacher's students outdistanced the other kindergarten classes both academically and socially. When the principal was asked what led her to make the new assignment, she responded that she sensed in the way that the teacher expressed her desire that this was a change that ought to be made. The teacher's past performance indicated that she could rise to the occasion. The leader's intuitive response allowed the teacher to expand her personal capacity and that of the school to meet the needs of the students.

COLLABORATION

Teaming is another important indicator of the principal's recognition that working in isolation is detrimental both to the accomplishment of the vision and to one's physical and emotional well-being. Successful leaders intuitively make decisions about what responsibilities should be delegated to team members. Leaders must be willing to take the risk of surrounding themselves with persons who are equally and, in some instances, uniquely qualified. One sign of an insecure leader is an underused administrative team.

One veteran high-profile principal is noted within the system for always hiring extremely competent coadministrators whose leadership styles are different yet complementary. This principal is also notorious, however, for not allowing his assistant principals (there have been a series) to take any actions without first receiving his permission. During an eight-year period, three of that person's assistants have accepted lateral transfers to other schools. In each case, when given expanded responsibilities, those persons have proven to be extremely competent.

That style of leadership is contrasts with that of a principal who has made a concerted effort to surround herself with a cadre of talented people whose skills complement or augment hers. Consequently, she has never had to turn down an opportunity for her school to benefit because of her fear of rising to a level of personal incompetence. Instead, she views herself as being as competent as the scope of the skills of her staff members.

PERSONAL AND POSITIONAL POWER

As they instinctively draw on lessons learned from the past, intuitive leaders legitimize an understanding of and commitment to the need to balance personal and positional power. Their experiences define sources of personal power as inclusive of the following:

- Image (appearance, grooming)
- Presentation skills (use of proper grammar, diction, and language appropriate to the audience)
- Competence (ability to provide direction and maximize staff effort to accomplish goals)
- Feedback (ability to give and receive constructive input)

In political organizations power is granted by the people over whom it will be exercised. . . . In the new organizations, titles and roles carry little weight until the leaders prove their competence. (Handy, 1996, p. 5)

Often, the exertion of positional power occurs at the expense of commitment. This is what traditionally happens within the military (Bridges, 1996). In initiating recruits, the training is built around reacting to positional power, with the goal being to acclimate subordinates to instantaneous response in support of a goal for which commitment and buy-in are not necessarily established. In school settings, total adherence to positional power is often manifested in teachers' seemingly overt compliance to dictates, policies, and/or procedures. "Compliance" ends, however, when, behind closed doors, those same teachers create their own minischools. They often brag about their ability to do the "real job" despite appearing to follow the leader.

When asked the question "How do you balance positional and personal power?" leaders overwhelmingly respond that it is necessary to engender real commitment from staff members to commonly shared goals. This recognition of the importance of commitment comes in reaction to the institution of increased standards of accountability, including changes in evaluation processes. Consequently, they see the continued need to move toward expanding opportunities for involving others in decision making.

> A principal shared that he didn't mind making the "tough on your feet, right now" health and safety decisions that had to be made. When time was not an issue, however, and the decision would affect more than one person, this principal sought to in some way consult with others. Leadership was viewed as an outgrowth of the examination of an issue from more than one perspective.

The use of positional power requires that the leadership position serve as a springboard for unleashing the personal power of all staff members. The context of leadership becomes much more inclusive. Yet this concept of the principal as politician is difficult for many leaders to accept. Previously, the expectation was that the politics of leadership would be visible at the level of the superintendent and the board of trustees, rather than at the level of principal and local school constituents. Typically, elected officials know that they must include within their speeches references to being empowered by the will of the people. The effective leader uses the word *we* in the context of "I am doing the work that we have agreed will be necessary to meet our goals for students."

The expansion of the leader's personal power becomes a natural outgrowth of the political approach to leadership. Subordinates respond to leadership that recognizes that perfect solutions do not rest within a position. In wielding personal power, the leader is freed to vary the way he or she interacts with individual staff members. The effort becomes directed more at achieving power through responding to and shaping the culture that exists within the organization. As the leader reads and accurately reacts to cultural clues, he or she develops a reputation for being able to make things happen. Yes, positional power can make things happen, but the issue is to what extent the subordinates are committed to the results that occur. As the leader begins to exert or rely on the value of personal power, that person will discover continuous opportunities to learn and to grow as a professional. The leader behavior reflects the understanding that sitting at the top of an unresponsive hierarchy makes that person an extremely vulnerable target.

> Another principal told of a time when, after a rather rocky year dealing with political issues within the community, she was called in by her superintendent. The superintendent debated either transferring her to a position at the central office or demoting her to an assistant principal. This experience led the principal to the intuitive realization that a leader is not invincible. This was the first time that she realized that her future as a principal was dependent on something other than positional power.

As the leader moves toward creating the necessary balance between personal and positional power within the political context, belief in oneself, a zealous approach to the goals embodied within the job, and a true respect for people become desirable attributes.

3

※

Powerful Communication

Reading the Silent Language

Communication dexterity is paramount to a leader's success. Conversely, difficulties with communication account for many of the structural, political, and human relation problems that are experienced by even the most seasoned educational leader. It is not just what the leader says that determines facility in the skill of communication. It is also an ability to know what not to say and when not to say it that contributes to overall communication savvy.

The purpose of this chapter is to look at some common forms of communication and how they affect a person's ability to intuit appropriate environmental cues:

- Listening
- Writing
- Body language
- Silence
- Speaking

LISTENING

The definition of listening includes the words "to list," which literally means to lean to one side. A person who is intent on understanding what someone else is saying will lean or be inclined toward the person—mentally, emotionally, and physically—to correctly interpret the sender's point of view. According to Richard Farson (1996) in his book *Management of the Absurd,* listening is less of a skill and more of an attitude, less of a technique but more of a genuine interest in what really matters to someone else.

> At her retirement celebration, a successful principal was showered with numerous accolades from staff, parents, and students. A theme that seemed to resonate throughout many of the comments was that she was a listener. When probed about this, she remarked that a mentor had suggested early on in her career that instead of simply "listening" for an opportunity to interject an opinion or "listening" to anticipate what to say next, one should "listen" not just to the words but to the intent.

The intuitive leader understands that success in reading environmental cues is often determined by the ability to hear not only the words but the intent that is being communicated.

The sophistication of the human brain poses a detriment to our ability to listen. The average rate of speech for many people is about 200 words per minute. The good news—and the bad news—is that the average person is able to think about four times that speed. The listener, with all that extra thinking time, may take advantage of little "side trips" to review yesterday's happenings, today's next steps, tomorrow's plans, or situational happenings that are peripheral to the two people speaking. Because of the speed of thought, one must consciously commit to listening. Choosing to listen challenges the brain to use that extra "think time" to focus more deeply on what the other person is trying to communicate. The listener must choose to ascertain from both the oral and unspoken messages the exact intent and desired response of the person talking.

> In an annual evaluation conference, an assistant principal received feedback that he needed to work on his listening skills. The assistant was especially surprised because this definitely was not the image that he held of himself. He asked a colleague from a neighbor-

ing school to shadow him for a half a day, noting his behavior especially when he was in situations in which he was called on to listen. He was surprised by the data that were shared with him. The colleague had noted that in several situations, mostly when he was in hallways or elsewhere on campus, the assistant principal occasionally diverted his eyes from the person with whom he was speaking to focus on people and/or events that were happening around him. When asked about this, the assistant principal acknowledged this as a conscious behavior on his part. He shared that he felt that his position required that he always be alert to his surroundings so that he could be on top of situations as they occurred. Yet he felt that he was still listening to the speaker and could repeat almost verbatim what had been said. Later, he reflected that it didn't matter if he "knew" he was listening. What mattered is that the speaker perceived that he was being listened to.

Leaders respond more intuitively when they learn the art of listening. Leaders must listen not just to the words but also for ideas and feelings. Listening beyond the spoken words will increase the ability to intuit what the appropriate response should be.

Listening can also be a disturbing experience. Through truly listening to another, a person runs the risk of seeing the world in a way that may be contrary to previously held perceptions. When listening is really happening—when a person is attempting to gain an understanding of another person's perspective—the listener is exposed to the risk of being changed. In essence, artful listening contributes to the intuitive leader's way of knowing.

WRITING

Understanding the power of written communication is another way to increase one's ability "to know." In trying to communicate an idea, a need, a compliment, or even a reprimand, it is common knowledge among managers that the written word can communicate a stronger message than the spoken word. With the written word, the typed message is considered to be more powerful than the one that is handwritten—even when the words are the same.

In an increasingly technological age, e-mail has facilitated the manner in which information is transmitted and received. For the leader, e-mail serves as a quick and easy means of communication.

The sender cannot always anticipate the context of when, where, and how an e-mail message is received, however. The intuitive communicator must be aware of this, as demonstrated in the following example:

> An assistant superintendent recently discovered the power of e-mail. Whether at home, at the office, or between meetings, she enjoyed being able to stay in touch with staff, principals, and others via technology. The ease of communicating through e-mail began to take precedence over more traditional ways of giving and getting information (e.g., phone calls, meetings, and face-to-face encounters). Although she felt more effective in getting daily tasks accomplished, she began to feel less and less connected to the people with whom she worked. She noticed that on several occasions, more was "read into" an e-mail message than she had intended or imagined. Further confirmation of her feelings came from an annual sentiment survey that was conducted. Feedback from employees, colleagues, and constituents indicated that she was efficient but impersonal. This evaluation was in contrast to results from a previous survey that had pointed to her "direct, but positive communication style." She commented that although she continues to use e-mail, she tries to "intuit" whether the message, request, compliment, admonishment, or simple relay of information will be better received through a less convenient but situationally more appropriate means of communication.

BODY LANGUAGE

The intuitive leader realizes that one of the most effective conduits for communication occurs nonverbally. Body language is manifested through eye movements, facial expressions, postural stances, and other small gestures. Through this mode of communication, leaders are able to relate interests, feelings, and cautions, as well as those beliefs and assumptions that may be more prone to surface via body language than through spoken word.

> An administrative intern who shadowed a superintendent for several weeks related what had been learned particularly about the leader's use of body language. Through direct observation, the intern noted how the leader would often nod his head when in con-

versation, rarely interrupting the speaker even when there was the proverbial "pregnant pause" in the midst of the interchange. Initially, the intern interpreted the head nodding as a sign of agreement, acceptance, or approval of what was being said. On questioning the superintendent about his behavior, the intern learned that the leader was quite aware of his head nodding. It was intentional, automatically done to signal listening, interest (not necessarily agreement), and permission to keep talking. When asked specifically about this behavior, the superintendent admitted that this was calculated to work to his advantage. People often ended up sharing much more information than perhaps was their initial intent—data that the superintendent was able to use in making decisions.

The numbers 90210 (a popular 1990s television show), 911 (the telephone number for emergencies), and 24/7 (slang for 24 hours, 7 days a week) are number combinations that are commonly understood by a large population of people. Wainright (1985) introduces the less recognized figures 07-38-55 as indicators of communication patterns. These numbers refer to the impact of a message in a face-to-face encounter. Of the impact, 7% is verbal, while 38% is related to nonverbal aspects of speech (i.e., volume, tone, pitch, voice quality, rate of speaking, accent, stress, nature and number of speech errors, etc.) and 55% of the impact has to do with body language. With 93% of the impact coming in the form of nonverbal communication, it makes a lot of sense for the leader to learn the importance and power of body language.

The intuitive leader learns that certain situations are addressed more effectively through body language as opposed to the spoken word. Sometimes, unspoken language can communicate what several hundred words may have difficulty explaining or when words simply just get in the way.

An assistant principal told of training parents to be campus monitors. She emphasized that not every situation requires a "get in their face/ream them out" response. Sometimes, standing near a group of students, not necessarily walking up to them, is a way to dissipate potentially negative behaviors. Students using foul language, in situations in which it is not directly aimed at a particular individual or group, can be stifled by the use of direct eye contact, a frown, a shaking of the head, or a finger to the lips. If the nonverbal communication is not seen or is ignored, then verbal intervention and subsequent actions may be necessary.

The intuitive leader uses space and proximity for communication purposes. In his book *The Silent Language,* Hall (1959) defined four zones in the use of space (see Table 3.1). The *intimate zone* is one in which people are actually touching or are easily able to touch each other. The second is the *personal zone* in which people are able to shake hands or are at most no more than an arm's length from each other. The third is the *social-consultive zone,* most commonly used in everyday encounters of a social or business nature. The final zone is the *public zone,* which is usually beyond 10 feet.

The intuitive leader uses environmental cues and files from the past to determine when these zones need to be respected or, if necessary, violated. In dealing with verbal displays of anger, the natural response is to increase proximal distance between the one listening and that of the person expressing anger. A successful strategy but a most uncomfortable plan of action (and perhaps dangerous if not in tune with both present and past experience) is to deliberately reduce the amount of space between the two parties. (It is important, however, not to move in too close, or the move will appear to be confrontational.) Often, the effect is that the angry person realizes, even on a subconscious level, that his or her comfort zone has been lessened, causing him or her to concentrate less on the words and emotions that are being relayed and more on the discomfort of someone entering personal space. This can divert the attention from the anger long enough to get the angry person focused on other, more constructive resolutions to the situation.

Finally, a smile is an extremely powerful form of nonverbal communication that often is taken for granted. Universally, the smile is accepted as an indicator of pleasure and happiness. The intuitive leader knows, however, that a smile can also be used in lieu of words to reassure, to relieve tension, or to reduce the effect of another person's attack.

SILENCE

Silence is rarely considered a form of communication, but it is. Silence communicates lots of things. Swets (1983) talks about the silence of *retreat,* which communicates a need to be alone, isolated with one's own thoughts. There is the silence of *anger,* which may be an attempt to get even or to lash out by keeping thoughts within.

Table 3.1 Zones of Personal Space

Zone	Range of Space	Definition
intimate	0 - 1.5 feet	actually touching or easily able to touch
personal	1.5 - 4.0 feet	able to shake hands or at least at arm's length
social-consultive	4.0 - 10.0 feet	used in everyday social or business encounters
public	10.0 feet +	within visual and hearing distance

SOURCE: Compiled from Hall (1959).

There is the silence of *awkwardness* that holds the message, "I don't know what to say" or "I'm waiting for someone else to say something." There is also the silence of *support,* which transmits the missive that the person is interested in listening without interrupting, giving advice, judging, or waiting until the speaker takes a breath so that opinions can be interjected.

> A superintendent told the story about a particularly trying board meeting at which a principal was taken to task about an incident that had occurred on a student field trip. The principal had been vilified in the local press and "beaten up" by several parents and community members. The principal, superintendent, and the board president were aware that the true story needed to remain confidential to protect the rights of the students involved and their families. Although the comments were harsh, the superintendent had communicated to the principal that issues of integrity made it necessary to remain resolute.
>
> The superintendent recalled sitting in the auditorium after the meeting. She took notice of how some colleagues avoided the principal, while others awkwardly offered, "Hang in there." Everyone had left. The superintendent remembered sitting down next to the principal and, for about three minutes, exchanging no words between them. Then, the superintendent got up, put her hand on the principal's shoulder, and said, "Have a good evening."
>
> After the truth about the incident had been revealed and the principal's reputation was once more intact, the superintendent and the principal met to reflect on the incident. The principal expressed appreciation of the silent companionship when he felt supported, understood, and cared about. He asked the superintendent, "How did you know?" She replied, "I just knew."

The intuitive leader is able to do an environmental read to determine when silence is the best vehicle for communicating what really needs to be said.

SPEAKING

In his book *The Art of Talking So That People Will Listen,* Swets (1983) lists several qualities that promote successful verbal communication: self-awareness, understanding, care for others, control of emotions, self- esteem, self-confidence, and sharing of oneself. He posits that although the conversational partner is an important factor in successful conversation, equally and sometimes more important is the person doing the speaking. The intuitive leader includes in his or her repertoire a compendium of skills and dispositions.

Self-awareness is cultivated by reflecting on the issue at hand and identifying the values, beliefs, and assumptions that cause one to hold a particular view. Although there needs to be a comfort with one's own views, needed also are an openness to new information and an ability to store it for later recall (files from the past).

> A high school dean of students related how she consistently needs to be mindful of showing preferential treatment to male students. Having grown up as the only female sibling among five older brothers, she remembered rarely being held accountable for her own "impish" behavior as a child because she was "a girl." Her siblings were inevitably accused of things when she was the culprit. As an administrator, she is confronted all day, every day, with situations requiring a high degree of sleuthing as well as intuition. She finds that she tends to listen with more sensitivity to her male students than do others in her same position.

Intuitive leaders are comfortably aware that they are not omniscient but are confident that the ideas, beliefs, and attitudes are worth sharing. Intuitive communicators also pay attention to their own behaviors and how verbal habits (e.g., interrupting and finishing another person's sentences) and nonverbal habits (e.g., lack of eye contact and staring) can irritate the listener.

Understanding requires a certain degree of feedback. In conversations, the intuitive leader seeks clarification about what is being said in an effort to stem misinterpretations and provide data to offset incorrect assumptions. The successful leader subscribes to the adage, "Seek not so much to be understood as to understand." Feedback helps avoid "pointless arguments, emotional explosions, and communication breakdowns" (Swets, 1983, p. 20). More often than not, the feedback comes in the form of nonverbal cues.

> An administrator of a large district shared about a period in his career when, reeling from the effects of a previous year's rather appealing retirement package, he was assigned to supervise 15 new

principals. Wanting to be more of a support to these new administrators, he tried to act as mentor to them in addition to being their supervisor. Unfortunately, it seemed that his intents were constantly misunderstood. Suggestions were interpreted as mandates. Offers to shadow principals and provide feedback were refused. His mere presence in some schools was met either with suspicion or with a noticeable degree of discomfort by the principal.

After several weeks of this, the administrator convened a focus group composed of six of the novices. A popular veteran principal was asked to facilitate the meeting. Specific feedback was solicited about how to better support these new site leaders. The district administrator purposely did not attend. Participants shared that although the principals liked and respected the administrator, it was never clear if he was acting in a supervisory or a mentoring mode. The confusion caused them to assume that even when he was acting as mentor, he was gathering data to use in their performance evaluations.

The district administrator used this information to persuade the superintendent to allow him to remain in the role of mentor while having someone else assume the duty of supervisor. Retired himself, this former administrator proudly tells anyone who will listen that all 15 of his protégés are still in the district and continue to meet with success.

Care for others is easily discerned by the person to whom one is speaking. Most people are readily able to determine if genuine caring is being expressed, even when there may be an attempt to feign concern. Their senses pick up clues from the choice of words, physical actions, facial expressions, and voice tone. When there is a feeling that someone does not really care, listening stops.

The successful leader intuitively knows that trust, the foundation that provides the basis for the connections formed between people, comes as a result of the following:

- Anticipating the emotional effects that decisions and actions might have on others
- Responding tactfully and respectfully in emotional situations
- Eliciting the perceptions, feelings, and concerns of others
- Recognizing that conflict is inevitable and using it to strengthen relationships
- Following through on commitments and keeping one's word

- Using the name of the other person when conversing with him or her
- Showing respect and courtesy
- Questioning, clarifying, and correcting others in a positive and professional manner
- Suggesting compromises
- Paraphrasing the speaker's views, feelings, and concerns
- Helping others save face when taking a different position (Muse, Sperry, Voelker, Harrington, & Harris, 1993, pp. 1-23)

Control of emotions is an essential skill that intuitive leaders develop and refine because they know that it is vital to maintaining effective communication. This does not mean that a person needs to be "emotionless"—desensitivity can be just as harmful as insensitivity. Intuitive leaders understand that an ability to read environmental cues requires them to keep perspective, not taking themselves too seriously. The challenge is to not underestimate the power of emotions that are engendered when negative responses are present, especially when they are directed against the leader.

An assistant principal tells of a conference in which he was lambasted by a parent angry about an incident that had occurred the previous day. The tone of the conference was combative, with the parent spewing comments and accusations without giving the administrator an opportunity to respond. Consciously suppressing the desire to verbally strike back, the assistant principal asked the parent, "What exactly is the outcome that you are seeking? Are you telling me all this because you want me to take a particular action, or do you just want me to listen and acknowledge that you are angry? And I definitely hear that you are angry." The parent stopped and said in a much calmer tone, "Nothing is going to change what happened. I just wanted someone to know how upset I am." The parent then exited the office but returned the next day to leave a note that said, "Thank you for letting me vent. I was not angry with you. Actually, I was angry with my child, myself, and the circumstances. It was kind of you to listen, considering the fact that I was not in the greatest of moods. Please accept my apologies." The assistant principal admitted that he had had to stifle his own anger. Intuitively, he knew that the best response was no response.

Self-confidence and *self-esteem* are not about egotism but rather about ego strength (Swets, 1983). Self-confidence and self-esteem allow one to be free of self-consciousness so that there can be more of an awareness and appreciation of others. If people detect that one values oneself, they are apt to act in a congruent manner. Self-confidence and self-esteem undergird a willingness to take risks and to courageously face people and situations that are new and different. Both of these attributes engender sincerity and integrity, not a need to project or protect false images. The leader who is able to create, rely on, and trust inner resources in all types of situations is the one who will find success in reading environmental cues and accessing files from the past.

A principal newly assigned to a historically low-achieving school talked about her first faculty meeting. The fourth principal in five years, she admittedly was a little nervous. She began her speech in the following way:

> "I was not sent here to be your fourth principal in five years. I chose to come here to be your principal, God willing, for many years to come. I feel that my prior experiences and training have prepared me for this new role. I believe that we are a match. But you must feel that it is a match, also, for us to do what I know we all want to do—improve student achievement."
>
> Three years later, achievement scores had begun to rise, but there were other indicators as well: Students were winning awards, teachers proudly announced that they were members of the faculty, and requests to transfer into the school had increased—both for students and staff. Says the principal, "I knew it was a match!"

Sharing of oneself suggests that words not only are a way to connect to other people but also are reflections of the speaker. Although no one is interested in hearing others talk on and on about themselves, people are interested in learning about a person's "real self." The intuitive leader understands that the act of sharing oneself invites others to share of themselves, which may result in deeper, more purposeful communication.

> A teacher was having some difficulty with classroom management. The assistant principal decided to share his own stories about discipline problems that he encountered when he first began to teach. During the next classroom observation, the assistant noticed a few changes in behavior on the part of the teacher. The changes seemed rather familiar, almost déjà vu. Conversations with the teacher

revealed that the personal sharing of the assistant principal had made her feel much more empowered to take appropriate actions. The teacher commented, "Now I know that it's OK not to be perfect."

The intuitive leader realizes that the sharing of self should not take on a competitive nature—one should not be conversing with "one-upmanship" as the goal. Competitive conversations are about winning (e.g., the strongest argument, the strongest tone, or who can sustain his or her argument for the longest time), not about deepening understanding.

SAYING NO

It is not uncommon for educational leaders to be put in the position of having to say "no" when someone wants a "yes." A strategy that intuitive leaders use, often without even being aware, is to cushion a negative response between statements of understanding and alternatives that can ease the sting of refusal:

a. I understand that this has been a long year for you and that you would like to take some vacation time.

b. Unfortunately, this is the first week of summer school, and I expect everyone to be here.

c. I have no problem approving your leave for the week before and/or the week after. I hope that this will work for you.

a. I understand that your child does not get along with her teacher and that you would like her to be transferred to another class.

b. My policy is to not transfer students this late in the semester. I will not approve a transfer.

c. I am more than willing to meet with your child and the teacher to pinpoint the problems, design solutions, and work toward making this a win-win experience for everyone involved—especially your child.

Intuitive leaders know that they always need to remain calm—even if is means temporarily taking leave of the situation to give all parties an opportunity to absorb what has been said, rethink positions, and/or "save face." It's not about acting in accordance with what others think but rather about acting according to standards that emerge from values and beliefs.

Effective communication is the major conduit for leaders who strive to use their intuitive skills. Being able to adequately and appropriately read the environment and access files from the past will be for naught without a recognition and a reliance on those communication tools (e.g., listening, writing, body language, silence, and speaking) that make for better relationships and increase the clarity and understanding of information—all the while enabling leaders to get to new and deeper levels of "knowing."

4

ꞏꞏꞏ

Intuition and the
Paradoxes of Leadership

Leaders constantly face the challenge of being called on in some way to initiate organizational change—a descriptor for the idea that all concepts, conditions, and creations constantly undergo some form of adaptation. On a daily basis, leaders face situations in which familiar solutions present themselves in unfamiliar terms requiring seemingly contradictory solutions. The concept, condition, or creation that could be defined and approached in a specific way today requires a different response a minute, an hour, or a day later. Consequently, leaders can benefit from heightening their awareness of the paradoxes of leadership. This awareness currently exists within the minds of leaders in the form of intuitive knowledge. Effective leaders have the ability to mentally access files from the past and to take environmental readings as sources for addressing issues that require them to act as change agents.

DEALING WITH PARADOXES

A state of constant alertness is required to intuit the best response to the many paradoxes of leadership. As leaders ponder and experiment with the best ways to solve problems, they remain vulnerable to the risk of having their intentions misinterpreted. Kotter (1998), however, reminds us that a characteristic behavior of leaders, as opposed to managers, is that they are risk takers driven by emotional, rather than rational, approaches to actualizing their vision. Consequently, leaders need to hold an expectation of being off-balance as a myriad of absurd paradoxes are encountered (Farson, 1996). Although the paradoxes of leadership have been the topic of research for a number of authors (Deal & Peterson, 1994; Farson, 1996; Kotter, 1998), the most prevalent paradoxes that surfaced are these:

- Leader Versus Manager
- Autocrat Versus Indecisive Decision Maker
- Facilitator Versus Obstructor
- Delegator Versus Leader-Centered Problem Solver

Included within this chapter are descriptions of how those paradoxes require intuitive responses from leaders.

LEADER VERSUS MANAGER

Current research on organizational development speaks to leadership and management functions. Depending on the author, the terms may be used interchangeably. For the purposes of this discussion, the two behaviors have been isolated.

Leadership

Leadership is closely associated with the ability to visualize, articulate, and create structures for supporting a vision for teaching and learning. This behavior relies on the skill of gaining the commitment of others. Leadership is essentially dynamic and heavily dependent on an ability to intuitively respond to those indicators of appropriate behaviors discerned from clues found in the environment. Effective leaders are astute at reading the environment. They recognize that despite the ever present opportunity to initiate change through the exertion of positional power, constituents will commit to making only those changes viewed as relevant, feasible, and worthy of trust.

Management

> If, in all of life, paradox is the rule and not the exception, as I believe it is, then the popular view of management as essentially a matter of gaining and exercising control is badly in need of correction. . . . Those who rely mainly on control are lost. (Farson, 1996, p. 38)

The related paradox is that as change agents, leaders cannot overlook the value of applying a management perspective to issues of change. By clarifying expectations, leaders increase the level of comfort and initiation at which constituents adapt to change. Structured management tools such as rules, regulations, and/or roles (Schlechty, 1997) clarify expected behaviors associated with a specific change effort. Unfortunately, a reliance on either leadership or management skills will not guarantee that the leader is free from criticism.

A principal related the story of being advised, as a novice principal, by his superintendent that the key to effectively moving a school toward academic excellence was to reduce most tasks to routines. By doing so, the superintendent postulated, the principal could best control the behaviors of staff members. The principal responded by formulating processes and procedures for everything from lesson plans to assemblies. A plethora of handbooks were created. Staff members were admonished of the consequences of failing to follow processes. Through time, the principal noted that although staff members overtly complied with procedures, the number of items on the agenda for his monthly meeting with the union increased. Visits to classrooms revealed that although teachers wrote beautiful plans, their instructional delivery did not demonstrate a passion for their work. Lessons were presented in a lackluster fashion. When students failed to meet standards, teachers pointed to their compliance with processes and procedures as a reason for placing the blame on students, rather than on their instruction.

As he intuitively read clues in the environment, the principal theorized that the lack of passion for teaching was connected to his failure to bridge for the teachers the paradox between his leadership and management approach to their work. He recognized the need to convey to the staff that structured management initiatives were not

> intended to replace their creativity, which had to be accessed to accomplish the vision of improvements in teaching and learning. He realized that the change visualized in student academic performance would require that he learn to meld leadership and management perspectives.

This principal intuited that managing change still required a recognition that staff members had to be provided with opportunities to commit to the leaders' "compelling vision" (Tichy & Devanna, 1990). He further recognized that leaders cannot mandate that which matters most—commitment (Fullan, 1993).

AUTOCRAT VERSUS INDECISIVE DECISION MAKER

A closely related paradox to leader versus manager is that of having actions viewed as either autocratic or indecisive. Leaders often complain that if they make decisions on their own, they're being autocratic. If they're open to the perspective of others, however, they're judged by constituents as too indecisive. The reality of leadership is that there will be times when change must be mandated. In those instances, allowing status quo behavior can be synonymous to malpractice. The leader must remain intuitively in tune to situations that require immediate action.

> A high school assistant principal tells of being appointed to a school in which students were constantly confronted with serious safety issues. The disorderly manner in which students were allowed to move about the building coupled with negative reactions to adult supervision were indicative of the absence of clear guidelines for acceptable behavior. The assistant principal decided that she couldn't wait for months to convene a discipline committee or to engage in debates about students' rights. Instead, acting by fiat, she identified (while mentally accessing files from the past) 10 incidents of misconduct that she deemed too dangerous to be ignored. As she read clues in the environment, she matched the offenses to a set of consequences for those student-valued activities (e.g., open campus and attendance at sporting events and dances). She noted that the reaction to her action was almost evenly split between those who championed her actions and those who complained that her approach was much too Machiavellian.

Too much inclusion was the lament of members of the administrative team at another school.

> A school leadership team's primary concern was that the principal was indecisive. The team joke was "How many administrative team members does it take to buy a ream of copy paper?" At this school, the principal viewed herself as exemplifying the attributes of an inclusive leader. Fortunately, the principal began to respond to subtle clues picked up during conversations with other staff members that indicated that she was not viewed as a decision maker. Because her ultimate intent had never been to abdicate decision-making authority, the principal intuitively became more judicious with regard to which issues to take before the administrative team.

Leaders must train themselves to trust their intuition. Intuition accessed as files from the past or in the form of environmental readings can be used to decide when and how to make decisions.

FACILITATOR VERSUS OBSTRUCTOR

A paradox that is often problematic for leaders is that of knowing when to act as facilitator versus obstructor. Facilitative leaders respect the abilities of staff members. Although remaining constant to a vision of optimum levels of student achievement, facilitative leaders pay close attention to the clues from staff members often expressed in the form of complaints of "what doesn't happen around here." Those leaders trust their ability to intuit the real issues that need to be addressed to support change.

> A principal noted that historically, efforts of teachers at her high school had gone without recognition. Opportunities to thank teachers for routinely providing services beyond those required in the union contract, such as extra hours spent in developing lessons, sponsoring clubs, and tutoring without pay, had been ignored. The principal began an incentive program that focused on teachers as well as on students. Staff began to receive notes of recognition for birthdays, anniversaries, and participation in courses or conferences. Opportunities to celebrate the accomplishments of students included recognition of teachers who contributed to the accomplishment. The presentation and wearing of celebratory T-shirts became a

vehicle for focusing on those values and beliefs that ultimately enhanced the learning environment. These acts of recognition created a climate of support.

Sometimes, the leader must intuit when there is a need to strategically obstruct actions. The leader carefully chooses those situations for which the correct response to the *why* of his or her reaction to a situation is an obstruction based on the rationalization "because I'm the leader."

Criteria for participation on the honor roll were the issue that led one principal to demonstrate "because I'm the leader" behavior. During a planning session to discuss marking period recognition with the school's incentive committee, the new principal was shocked to hear that students who received a check mark on the conduct section of the student report card could not be included on the honor roll. Immediately, the principal stated that this identification process was in direct opposition to his personal values and beliefs about recognizing student success. As he accessed files from the past, he surmised that this process was probably particularly unfair to male students. He recalled that during the marking period, even some of his brightest young men had at least one referral on file in the disciplinarian's office. He further recognized that young men's behavior tended to be less inhibited than that of young women. The principal's position was that the proper way to acknowledge the students' infractions was to deny them recognition under the category of good citizenship. The committee was not happy with the mandate. The guidelines for recognition for the honor roll, however, were subsequently changed to reflect the deeply held values and beliefs of the principal.

DELEGATOR VERSUS LEADER-CENTERED PROBLEM SOLVER

Leaders recognize the payoff to be garnered from facilitating the involvement of others in decision making. They go a step further, however. They recognize the value inherent in sharing responsibility for implementation. They are guided by the question, "What is the task and who should be doing the work?" The major challenge is to make decisions and then to prioritize the need to personally be involved in tasks and/or decisions.

The daily life of a principal is characterized by "brevity, variety, and fragmentation" (Peterson, 1997). A leader's life is characterized by almost incredible variances in demands. Here are some excerpts from a principal's account of a typical day.

7:00 a.m.	Arrived at school.
7:04 a.m.	Placed cellular call to the pager of the head custodian to describe problem with front door keypad.
7:20 a.m.	Took a call from parent of child who was threatened on the way home from school by a child from another school.
7:26 a.m.	Spoke to secretary who called to say that her lights were out because of last night's storm. She can't come in to work.
7:42 a.m.	Received call from teacher who would be absent and can't get through to the substitute center.
7:45 a.m.	Finally, opened the door to personal office.
7:49 a.m.	Received another call from a teacher who will be absent. Reported that sub center says that there are no more substitutes available.
7:54 a.m.	Heard complaint from department chairperson that the clerk refuses to distribute supplies except on Thursdays.
8:00 a.m.	Observed the assistant principal arriving, getting his mail, and going upstairs to meet with a teacher.
8:17 a.m.	Took call from the school site council chairperson about the need to schedule a budget committee meeting.
8:26 a.m.	Met with science teacher regarding permission needed to schedule a special field trip to Super World Amusement Park.
8:42 a.m.	Talked to a parent and a child about problems with proper use of the Internet in the media center.
8:46 a.m.	Added the media center director to the conversation.

8:48 a.m.	Interrupted by call from the district office regarding missing school safety plan.
9:00 a.m.	Used the P.A. system to greet students and staff with daily announcements, reminders, and celebratory news.
9:07 a.m.	Auditor arrived to begin surprise audit of lunch applications, attendance books, and payroll documents.
9:10 a.m.	Called secretary to beg her to come in.
9:16 a.m.	Left the office to check the corridors for tardy students.
9:35 a.m.	Paged over the intercom by the school nurse.
9:39 a.m.	Discussed with the school nurse a student who has obvious bruises on her face. Child said that her mother slapped her that morning for taking too long to get dressed for school. Possible child abuse indicated.
10:02 a.m.	Placed call to Department of Children and Family Services.
10:14 a.m.	Had conference with child sent to the office for swearing at the teacher.
10:35 a.m.	Received call back from the social worker from Department of Children and Family Services.
10:50 a.m.	Accepted call from teachers' union representative regarding pending grievance hearing.
11:02 a.m.	Received call from representative of the State Board of Education regarding scheduling of biannual quality review visit.
11:15 a.m.	Frantic visit from seventh-grade social studies teacher reporting a downed Internet connection —e-mail conversation with sister school in France has been interrupted.
11:46 a.m.	Counseled lunchroom manager who is upset because the catering service that provides the meals keeps sending the vegetables that she told them that the students hate.
11:50 a.m.	Received call from principal of neighboring school about scheduling an administrative committee meeting.
12:00 p.m.	Met with parent who came in to request special education screening.

12:16 p.m.	Visited with publisher's representative who stopped by hoping to have a few moments to introduce her latest reading series.
12:30 p.m.	Greeted substitute secretary who has never been assigned to a school site.
12:35 p.m.	Called district office to speak with bilingual education coordinator.
1:10 p.m.	Observed in sixth-grade classroom of a new teacher.
1:43 p.m.	Representative from Department of Children and Family Services made an unscheduled appearance to take custody of a family of children. (She reports that she was not assigned to a.m call—"That's someone else's jurisdiction.")
2:11 p.m.	Began to review results from state testing program review with school counselor.
2:22 p.m.	Visited a seventh-grade classroom to discuss rumors of impending fight.
2:41 p.m.	Local real estate agent called requesting a copy of summary information related to test scores.
2:55 p.m.	Took a bite out of sandwich.
3:00 p.m.	Made intercom announcement to congratulate math competition winner.
3:15 p.m.	Mingled with students and parents during dismissal.
3:55 p.m.	Received a call from the husband of a staff member who is upset about their pending divorce.
4:11 p.m.	Responded to a fax from the district.
4:35 p.m.	Returned call to the local park district about scheduling swimming lessons.
5:00 p.m.	Attended and served as speaker for the regular monthly meeting of the Chamber of Commerce.
7:15 p.m.	Came back to school to participate in PTA meeting.
10:30 p.m.	Finally at home, began reading an article in preparation for tomorrow's meeting of doctoral cohort.

A day such as this demonstrates the need for principals to know when to delegate the authority needed to effectively address the "brevity, variety, and fragmentation" of the job so that they can remain focused on achieving the vision for teaching and learning.

The extent to which leaders involve staff in decision making is both site specific and related to that person's administrative style. In the previous scenario, several incidents could have been delegated:

- A parent volunteer could have been asked to run the office for the day.
- The assistant principal could have handled substitutes and the Department of Children and Family Services.
- The teacher with the Internet problem could have been referred to school or district technology coordinator.
- A teacher could have been assigned to serve as a state quality review coordinator.
- A rotating schedule of students could have been used to make daily announcements. (Teachers could coordinate the schedule.)
- Publisher representative could have met with textbook committee chairperson.

It is not unusual for leaders to mask personal feelings or levels of insecurity by assuming a more exclusive than inclusive approach to leadership. Facilitative leaders intuitively acknowledge the value of maintaining a relationship with staff that is more collaborative than directive. They demonstrate through the delegation of authority evidence of their belief that staff members are capable of providing solutions to problems that affect their professional lives. When put into place, a number of practices will facilitate staff involvement in decision making while protecting the rights of the leader (Carothers, 1995).

Leaders must provide opportunities for both themselves and their constituents to become skilled in problem solving and decision making. It is important that issues be addressed in a systematic manner. Sharing of information empowers not only staff members but also leaders. Research (Belasco & Stayer, 1993) indicates that employees are more likely to work toward meeting those organizational targets for which they have a background of related data. All members of the school community need to be armed with an understanding of goals and the data needed to make decisions that influence achieving the desired outcome.

In the absence of the presence of the leader, many staff members have internalized through observation the leader's overriding values and beliefs. Consequently, those staff members may be conditioned to apply the leader's preferred approach to addressing an issue. Leaders need to be aware that how they empower their staff members through training is critical to creating and maintaining a climate that can support the delegation of authority.

Intuitive leaders understand the importance of and benefits that result from creating collaborative climates where both debate and creative approaches to problem solving are encouraged. They understand the need to establish parameters within which the decision-making authority can be delegated to staff members or committees. They clearly define boundaries, so that staff members trust that they are making decisions in areas that will effect change. Leaders must recognize that when authority is delegated, their own credibility and, consequently, their effectiveness are enhanced.

Using the tools of intuition via environmental readings and files from the past offers the benefit of expanded ranges of solutions to problems for those leaders working to actualize their visions for student success.

References

Agor, W. (1984). *Intuitive management.* Englewood Cliffs, NJ: Prentice Hall.

Agor, W. (1986). *The logic of intuitive decision making.* Englewood Cliffs, NJ: Prentice Hall.

Armstrong, T. (1998). *Awakening genius in the classroom.* Alexandria, VA: Association for Supervision & Curriculum Development.

Belasco, J. A., & Stayer, R. C. (1993). *Flight of the buffalo soaring to excellence: Learning to let employees lead.* New York: Warner Books.

Bridges, W. (1996). Leading the de-jobbed organization. In F. Hesselbein, M. Goldsmith, & R. Beckhard (Eds.), *The leader of the future.* San Francisco: Jossey-Bass.

Carothers, J. (1995). *Participatory decision making: Principals' perceptions and teachers' perceptions.* Unpublished doctoral dissertation, University of Illinois at Urbana.

Day, L. (1997). *Practical intuition.* New York: Broadway Books.

Deal, T., & Peterson, K. (1994). *The leadership paradox: Balancing logic and artistry in schools.* San Francisco: Jossey-Bass.

Deal, T., & Peterson, K. (1999). *Shaping school culture: The heart of leadership.* San Francisco: Jossey-Bass.

Dean, D., & Mihalsky, J. (1974). *Executive ESP.* Englewood Cliffs, NJ: Prentice Hall.

Emery, M. (1994). *Dr. Marcia Emery's intuition workbook: An expert's guide to unlocking the wisdom of your subconscious mind.* Englewood Cliffs, NJ: Prentice Hall.

Farson, R. (1996). *Management of the absurd: Paradox in leadership.* New York: Simon & Schuster.

Fullan, M. (1993). *Change forces: Probing the depths of educational reform.* New York: Falmer.

Hall, E. T. (1959). *The silent language.* New York: Doubleday.

Handy, C. (1996). The new language of organizing and its implications for leaders. In F. Hesselbein, M. Goldsmith, & R. Beckhard (Eds.), *The leader of the future.* San Francisco: Jossey-Bass.

Kotter, J. P. (1998, Fall). Winning at change. *Leader to Leader, 10,* 27-34.

Muse, I., Sperry, D., Voelker, M., Harrington, P., & Harris, D. (1993). Interpersonal sensitivity. In S. Thomas (Ed.), *Principals for our changing schools.* Fairfax, VA: National Policy Board for Educational Administration.

Peterson, K. (1997). [Video]. Presentation to the Chicago Academy for School Leadership, Chicago.

Rosanoff, N. (1991). *Intuition workout: A practical guide to discovering and developing your inner knowing.* Fairfield, CT: Aslan.

Schein, E. H. (1996). Leadership and organizational change. In F. Hesselbein, M. Goldsmith, & R. Beckhard (Eds.), *The leader of the future.* San Francisco: Jossey-Bass.

Schlechty, P. C. (1997). *Inventing better schools: An action plan for educational reform.* San Francisco: Jossey-Bass.

Schön, D. (1989). Professional knowledge and reflective practice. In T. J. Sergiovanni & J. H. Moore (Eds.), *Schooling for tomorrow: Directing reform to issues that count.* Boston: Allyn & Bacon.

Swets, P. (1983). *The art of talking so that people will listen: Getting through to family, friends, and business associates.* New York: Simon & Schuster.

Tichy, N. M., & Devanna, M. (1990). *The transformational leader.* New York: John Wiley.

Vaughan, F. E. (1979). *Awakening intuition.* New York: Anchor.

Wainright, G. R. (1985). *Body language.* Lincolnwood, IL: NTC Contemporary.

Index